easy piano
Smash
annual 2002

GW00692094

Published 2002

Editor: Chris Harvey
Cover Design: Space DPS Limited

International
MUSIC
Publications

© International Music Publications Limited
Griffin House 161 Hammersmith Road London W6 8BS England

All You Want

words and music by
Dido Armstrong, Paul Herman and Rollo Armstrong

highest chart position not eligible for chart entry
release date 10th December 2001
did you know Dido co-wrote the track "I'm Not A Girl, Not Yet A Woman" for Britney Spears' latest album Britney

I like to watch you sleep at night, to hear you breathe, by my ___ side.

And al-though sleep leaves me be-hind, ___ there's no-where I'd ra - ther be. ___

And now our bed is oh, so cold, my hands feel emp-ty. No one to hold. ___
(See block lyric)

It's been three years, one night apart
But in that night you tore my heart
If only you had slept alone
If those seeds had not been sown
Oh, you could come home
And you would know that

All you want
Is right here in this room
All you want
And all you need
Is sitting here with you
All you want

Anything Is Possible

highest chart position 1
release date 25th February 2002
did you know Advance sales of the 'Evergreen'/'Anything Is Possible' double a-side came in at 1.2 million – a figure which proved conservative when the single went on to sell a staggering 1.1 million copies within six days of release

words and music by
Cathy Dennis and Chris Braide

Mmm_____ Oh_____ Yeah___

I nev-er thought I could be feel-ing this way,___ stand - ing here in front of you___
(See block lyric)

this per-fect day,___ no. It's hard to i-ma-gine where to-mor-row will_ lead.___ I'll keep

nev-er will doubt it a-gain, I'm fly-ing___ high,_____ 'cause your love's made me see___ that a-

-ny-thing is pos-si-ble,___ it's pos-si-ble_ when you be-lieve in, a-ny-thing is pos-si-ble,

pos-si-ble, when you be-lieve in me,_____ me._____ When you be-lieve in_____ me._

In a world full of strangers
You were my saving grace
You told me I was not alone
Alone in this place
No I never believed it
That a dream can come true
But if anyone has changed my mind
Then baby it's you

Can't Get You Out Of My Head

words and music by
Cathy Dennis and Robert Davis

highest chart position 1
release date **17th September 2001**
did you know **Before Kylie hit the big-time
she worked in a video rental shop**

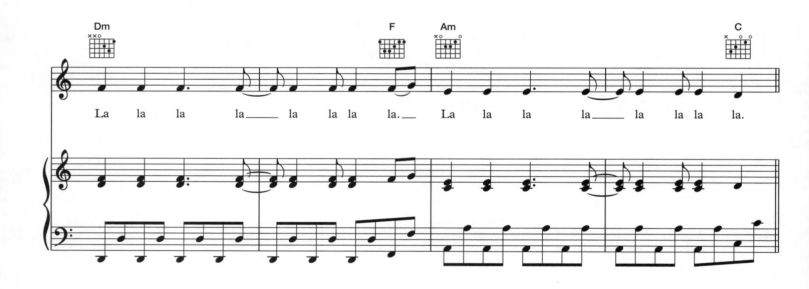

La la la la___ la la la la. La la la la___ la la la la.

La la la la___ la la la la. La la la la___ la la la. I just

There's a dark secret in me
Don't leave me locked in your heart
Set me free
Feel the need in me
Set me free
Stay forever and ever and ever and ever

Complicated

words and music by
**Lauren Christy, Graham Edwards
Scott Spock and Avril Lavigne**

highest chart position 3
release date **26th August 2002**

did you know As a child, Lavigne progressed from singing on
her bed, imagining an audience of thousands, to playing at country
music festivals and showcases. But it was R&B legend Antonio 'LA'
Reid who gave her a break and signed her to Arista Records

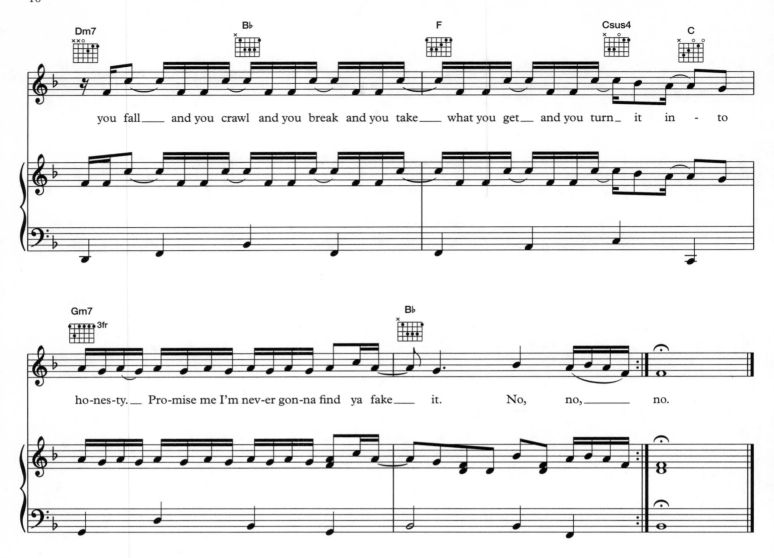

you fall___ and you crawl and you break and you take___ what you get___ and you turn_ it in - to

ho-nes-ty.___ Pro-mise me I'm nev-er gon-na find ya fake___ it. No, no,_____ no.

Chill out
Watcha yelling for?
Lay back
It's all been done before
And if you could only let it be
You will see somebody else 'round ev'ryone else
You're watching your back like you can't relax
You're try'n' to be cool
You look like a fool to me

DJ

words and music by
Graham Stack and Paul Rein

highest chart position **3**
release date **6th May 2002**

did you know H & Claire are a duo drawn from the ashes of teen pop sensation Steps. After the band's demise they were both offered recording contracts but, as they confessed, "we were just too chicken to do it on our own!"

Ooh___ eh_____ Ooh___ eh___

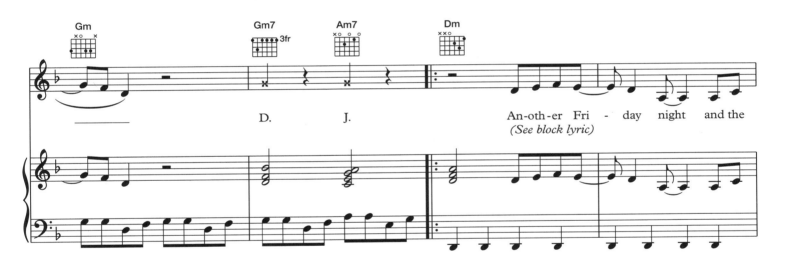

___ D. J.

An-oth-er Fri - day night and the
(See block lyric)

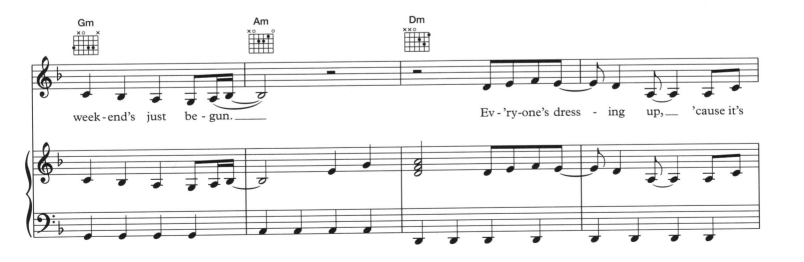

week-end's just be - gun.___ Ev-'ry-one's dress - ing up,___ 'cause it's

Everyone's feeling good
Smiling faces everywhere
So if you're in the mood
Put your hands up in the air

Tonight, live all your fantasies
Tonight, playing it on and on

Don't Let Me Get Me

highest chart position 6
release date 13th May 2002
did you know Another single from her mega-successful *Mizzundaztood* album, this track features a themed video which follows Pink back to her high school, before she's promised pop stardom in exchange for "changing everything you are"

words and music by
Alecia Moore and Dallas Austin

Ne-ver win first place, I don't sup-port the team.

I can't take di-rec - tion and my socks are ne-ver___ clean. Tea - chers dat - ed me,___

my___ pa-rents hat - ed me,_ I was al - ways in a fight, 'cause I can't do no-thing right.

Ev - 'ry-day I fight a war___ a-gainst the mir-ror. I can't take the per - son star-ing back

Falling

words and music by
Bernard Butler and David McAlmont

highest chart position **23**
release date **29th July 2002**

did you know In the mid-90s McAlmont and Butler had the critics drooling over their unexpected nouveau Motown. Then they fell apart and made some fairly pointed remarks about each other. Happily, just like a Home Counties version of Sam and Dave, they're back wowing the critics again

♩ = 118

Feel - ing lost___ and I___ don't wan - - na be here,_____
(See block lyric)

burn-ing up___ in - side_ the at - - mos-phere._____   If I_ should spread

__ my   wings, I could fly_____ a - way,_____   but I don't_____ wan-na stay

fall - - ing for you._____ Ah,___ yeah,

_____ fall - ing for you.____

See the world below and I'm floating by
All alone here in the fearless sky
Feeling weightless, please don't let me go
'Cos I need you so here tonight
Tonight

Freak Like Me

highest chart position 1
release date 22nd April 2002
did you know The Sugababes are a trio of Keisha, Mutya and Heidi. Heidi is the newest member, who was in the original formation of Atomic Kitten in her native Liverpool, while Keisha and Mutya had been signed to a record deal aged only 14 before they hit with the single 'Overload'

words and music by
Gary Numan, Eugene Hanes, Marc Valentine, Loren Hill, William Collins, George Clinton and Gary Cooper

Let me lay it on the line, I got a lit-tle freak-i-ness in-side, and you know that a man has got-ta deal with it. I don't care what they say, I'm not a-bout to pay no-bo-dy's way, 'cause it's all a-bout the dog in me. I wan-na

Girlfriend

words and music by
**Chad Hugo, Pharrell Williams
and Justin Timberlake**

highest chart position 2
release date 15th April 2002

did you know Singers Justin Timberlake and J.C. Chasez once co-starred in the Disney Channel's *The Mickey Mouse Club*. Their success in the late 90s with singles like 'I Want You Back' and 'Tearing Up My Heart' was built on a tour of roller rinks

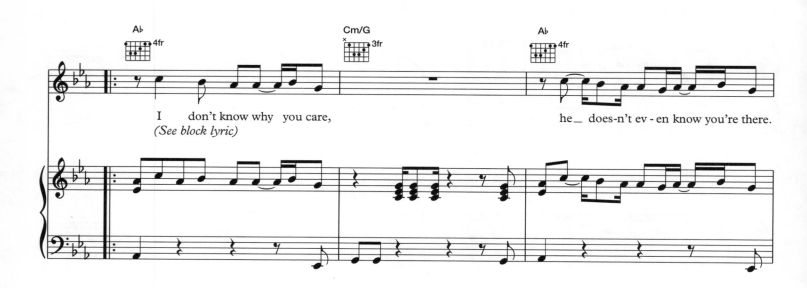

I don't know why you care,
(See block lyric)

he_ does-n't ev - en know you're there.

'Cause he don't love your eyes

and he don't love your smile.

Does he know what you feel?
Are you sure that it's real?
Does he ease your mind
Or does he break your stride?
Did you know that love could be a shield?

Handbags And Gladrags

words and music by
Mike D'Abo

highest chart position 4
release date **26th November 2001**
did you know **Among other things, the Stereophonics
are famed for being the first ever signing to
Richard Branson's new music label, V2 Records**

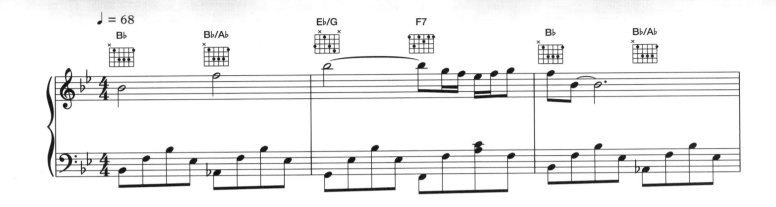

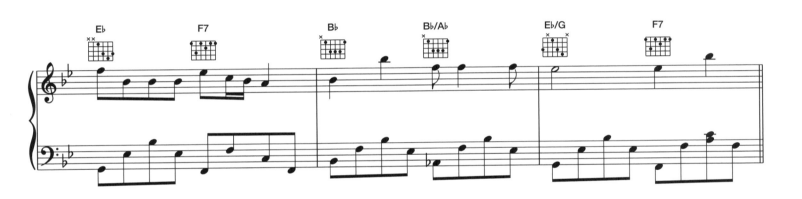

Ev-er see a blind man cross the road ___
(See block lyric)

try'n' to make the oth-er side? _____

throw them all __ a-way,   the hand-bags and the glad - rags that your poor __ old gran-dad had to sweat to buy

__ you.

Once I was a young man
And all I thought I had to do was smile
Well you are still a young girl
And you bought everything in style
So once you think you're in, you're out
'Cause you don't mean a single thing
Without the handbags and the gladrags
That your poor old grandad
Had to sweat to buy you

Have You Ever

words and music by
Andrew Frampton, Cathy Dennis and Christopher Braide

highest chart position **1**
release date **Monday 19th November 2001**
did you know S Club 7 enlisted the help of 250,000 school children in the recording of this year's Children In Need single. Pupils from 5000 schools took part in the final cut which promises to break the record for the most people singing on a single

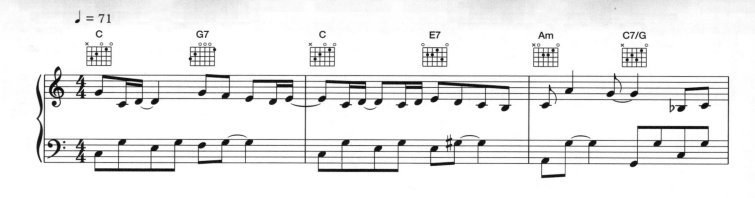

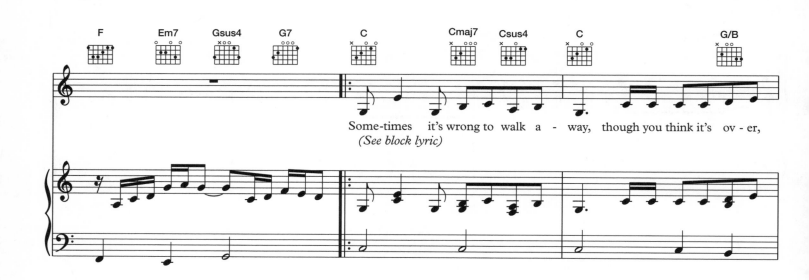

Some-times it's wrong to walk a - way, though you think it's ov - er,
(See block lyric)

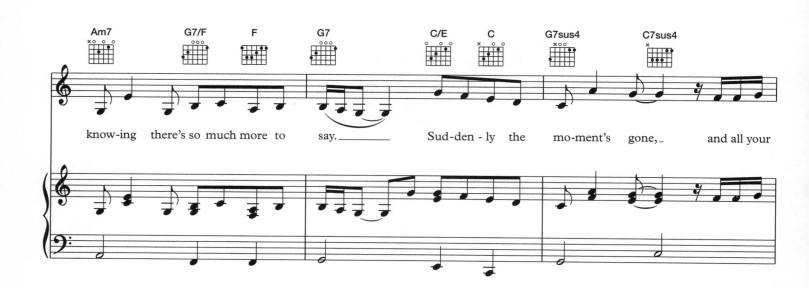

know-ing there's so much more to say._____ Sud-den - ly the mo-ment's gone,__ and all your

loved and lost the day___ I let,___ yes I loved and lost___ the day___ I let,___ yes I

loved and lost the day___ I let you go._____

Can't help but think that this is wrong
We should be together
Back in your arms where I belong
Now I've finally realised
It was forever that I'd found
I'd give it all to change the way
The world goes round

Hero

words and music by
Enrique Iglesias, Paul Barry and Mark Taylor

highest chart position 1
release date 21st January 2002
did you know Enrique's cultural favourites include Ernest Hemingway, *Pinnocchio* and *Bugs Bunny*. He also loves lettuce. Unsurprisingly for a man with the genes of dad Julio, his favourite magazine reading is industry bible *Billboard*

(*Spoken*) Let me be your hero. Would you dance if I asked you to dance? Would you run and ne-ver look back? Would you cry if you saw me cry-ing? Would you save my soul to-night? Would you

You can take my breath a - way. Oh,____ I just want to hold you.

I just want to hold you, oh yeah. Am I in too deep? Have I lost my

mind? Well I don't care you're here to - night.____

I can be your he - ro ba - by. I can kiss a - way the pain.

How You Remind Me

highest chart position 4
release date 11th February 2002

did you know Nickelback started life as a cover band in Calgary, before singer Chad Kroeger borrowed $4000 from his stepfather and moved to Vancouver to cut some demos. While waiting for his break he spent two years selling advertising space for a football magazine. He used his PR knowledge to get his friends to fax radio stations to help get airplay for Nickelback's first single

words and music by
Chad Kroeger, Michael Kroeger, Ryan Peake and Ryan Vikedal

Ne-ver made it as a wise man, *(See block lyric)* I could-n't cut it as a poor man steal-in'.

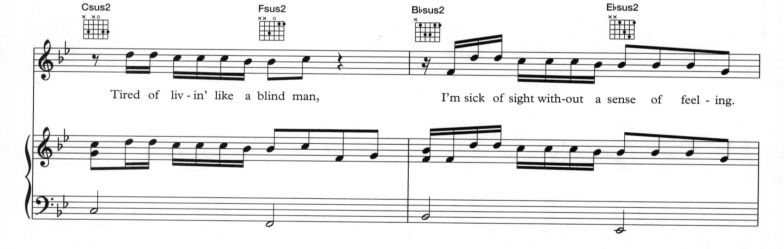

Tired of liv-in' like a blind man, I'm sick of sight with-out a sense of feel-ing.

omit 2nd time

And this is how____ you re-mind____ me.

It's not like you didn't know that
I said I love you and swear I still do
And it must have been so bad
'Cause livin' with me must have damn near killed you
This is how you remind me of what I really am
This is how you remind me of what I really am

I Love It When We Do

highest chart position 5
release date 8th September 2002
did you know He's only 25, but he's already sold 14 million albums. Since establishing himself, Ronan's been hobnobbing with rock's aristocracy, interviewing David Bowie, duetting with Elton John, and even hosting the *Eurovision Song Contest* and *Miss World*.

words and music by
Gregg Alexander and Rick Nowels

I love it when we do what we do when we do, I love it when we

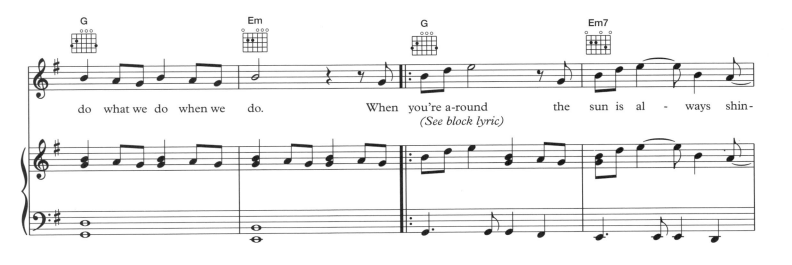

do what we do when we do. When you're a-round the sun is al - ways shin-
(See block lyric)

- ing, and since we met I have-n't once__ stopped smil-

When you're around my eyes will never wander
And no one else, I've ever been more fonder of
So baby don't break the spell I'm under
Yeah
When I look into your eyes
I don't have to fantasise
You're a dream that's realised
Dancing on the moon inside
If life is cruel then someone lied
Yeah

I Want Love

words by **Bernie Taupin**
music by **Elton John**

highest chart position 9
release date 24th September 2001
did you know In 1992, Elton broke Elvis Presley's old record for the most consecutive years of Top 40 hits on Billboard's singles chart, having had a continual presence every year since the late 1970 entry of "Your Song"

I want love____ but it's im - pos - si - ble,____ a man like me's____ so ir - re -

- spon - si - ble.____ A man like me is dead in pla - ces

If You Come Back

highest chart position 1
release date 12th November 2001
did you know Apparently the band are all elephant lovers and care for injured mammals in their spare time . . .

words and music by

Ray Ruffin, Nicole Formescu, Ian Hope and Lee Brennan

I watched you go
Taking my heart with you
Oh yes you did
Every time I tried to reach you on the phone
Baby you're never there
Girl you're never home
So if I did something wrong please tell me
I wanna understand
'Cos I don't want this love to ever end

I'm Alive

words and music by
Andreas Carlsson and Kristian Lundin

highest chart position **17**
release date **19th August 2002**
did you know 'No, you're not'. That was the unkind response made by one reviewer to this single's title, and the Canadian songstress certainly invites castigation from the more sniffy members of the musical community. But you can't argue with record sales, and Dion remains a diva numero uno in the pop world.

When you call on me, when I hear you breathe,

I get wings to fly. I feel_____ that__ I'm a-

-live. When you look at me, I can

I'm Not A Girl, Not Yet A Woman

words and music by
Dido Armstrong, Max Martin and Rami Jacoub

highest chart position 2
release date **1st April 2002**

did you know **In 2001 Britney launched her new video game 'Britney's Dance Beat', on Game Boy Advance – the latest in a list of endorsements that includes Pepsi. Britney features throughout the game as a very strict dance instructor**

I used to think___

(See block lyric)

I had the an - swers to ev -

- 'ry-thing.

But now I know_____ that

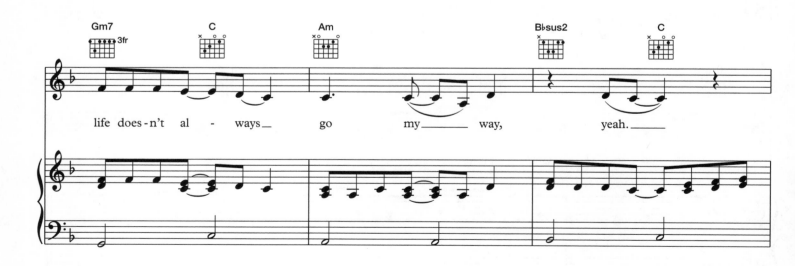

life does-n't al - ways___ go my_____ way, yeah.___

I'm not a girl
There is no need to protect me
It's time that I learn to face up to this on my own
I've seen so much more than you know now
So don't tell me to shut my eyes

Just A Little

words and music by
**Michelle Escoffery, John Hammond-Hagan
and George Hammond-Hagan**

highest chart position 1
release date **13th May 2002**
did you know **Liberty X are Michelle, Jessica, Kelli,
Kevin and Tony – the "other" five finalists from TV's *Pop Stars*.
They were originally titled Liberty until and American band of the
same name complained**

work it a lit-tle, get hot, just a lit-tle, meet me in the mid-dle, let go just a lit-tle bit more.

Just a lit-tle bit, give me just a lit-tle bit more.___ Give me just a lit-tle bit___ more. (Just a lit-tle).

repeat ad lib. to fade

Let me, I do anything if you just let me
Find a way to make you respond
I know you wanna break down those walls
Oh yeah, yeah
And it's so challenging
Getting close to you's like I'm imagining
I just wanna see you get down
You gotta let it all out

Lovin' Is Easy

words and music by
Kelly Levesque and David Eriksen

highest chart position 6
release date 26th August 2002

did you know Aside from jokes about a certain member's resemblance to pixelated troll Shrek, Hear'Say have also had to endure regular accusations that their career is about to peter out after a trailblazing entrance. Whether it does or not is said to hinge largely on the success of this comeback single.

Ooh__ ooh__

Ooh__ ooh__   When I'm a-lone,   I can-not help my-self from
(See block lyric)

fall-ing deep-er in love   with you.____ Mm   hold-ing you close

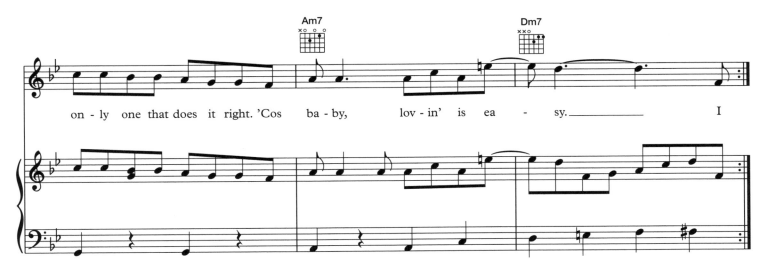

on - ly one that does it right. 'Cos ba - by, lov - in' is ea - sy. _____ I

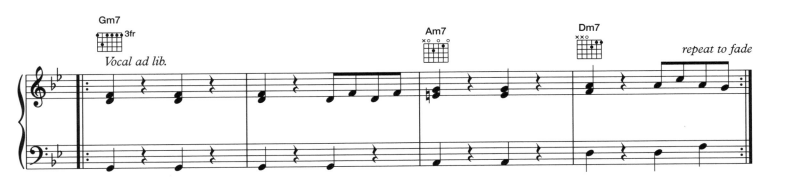

Vocal ad lib.

repeat to fade

Touching your skin
I want to have you to myself boy
Only want you
Everything you say
It means so much to me
You are my life, my love and my one

A Mind Of Its Own

words and music by
**Andrew Frampton, Victoria Beckham
and Steve Kipner**

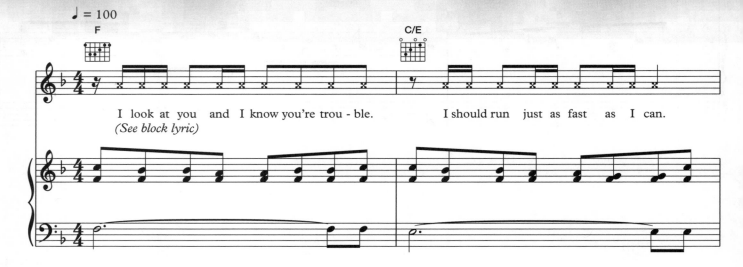

highest chart position **6**
release date **4th February 2002**

did you know **Victoria Beckham and hubby David make a cameo
appearance in *Bend It Like Beckham*, a film
documenting a young Indian woman's dream of
playing professional football, which featured
look-alikes of the couple**

♩ = 100

I look at you and I know you're trou - ble.
(See block lyric)
I should run just as fast as I can.

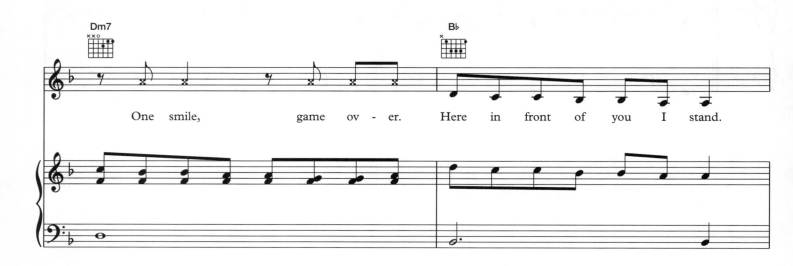

One smile, game ov - er. Here in front of you I stand.

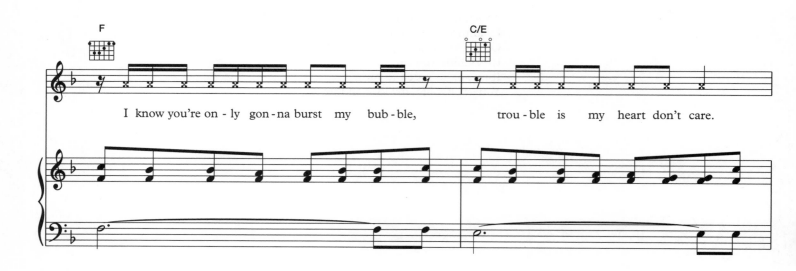

I know you're on - ly gon - na burst my bub - ble, trou - ble is my heart don't care.

take. Does-n't it know_ that I____ get hurt____ too, when it acts__ that way.
My

repeat ad lib. to fade

heart's got a mind of its own.

My

Too many times I witnessed
My heart make a fool of itself
So sure it's gonna turn out one way
Always turns out being something else
My heart's got a real malfunction
Always flipping into over-ride
When I tell it to be sensible
It over-rules my cynical mind
I'm not willing to be so open
Transparent, no, not yet
(Once bitten, twice shy)
Is what you get

Point Of View

highest chart position 3
release date 18th February 2002

did you know Italian dance act DB Boulevard feature the voice of Venetian Moony. And while the group fought it out with Victoria Beckham for the number one spot (only for both to be beaten by Enrique Iglesias), Moony revealed that she was good friends with Spiller, who beat Mrs Beckham to the number one spot back in 2000 with 'Groovejet'

words and music by
Monica Bragato, Alfredo Comazzetto, Thomas Croquet, Christian Mazzalai, Laurent Mazzalei and Frederic Moulin

Don't have a cent,___ will I pay my rent?

And ev - en my car does - n't work.

I see birds and trees
All the flowers of the world
So beautiful
Won't you come with me

People Get Ready

words and music by
Curtis Mayfield

highest chart position has not charted at time of publication
release date 4th March 2002
did you know Cassidy spent several years working as a backing singer before she was struck down by cancer in 1996, just as she began earning recognition. She'd originally put the pain in her hip down to all the ladder work she'd been doing while painting murals in school cafeterias

Peo-ple get rea-dy,___ there's a train a-com-in', you don't need no bag-gage, you just get on board.___ All you need is faith___ to hear die-sels a-hum-min',

- pen the doors and board them, there's room for all_____ of the loved_ and lost. A-yeah.

Electric Guitar Solo

Now there ain't no room_____ for the hope - less sin-ner,_____

Soak Up The Sun

highest chart position 16
release date 1st April 2002

did you know Crow is one of the most celebrated of a new generation of American singer-songwriters, counting Keith Richards of the Rolling Stones, the Dixie Chicks, Chrissie Hynde and Eric Clapton among her fans. Indeed, all of those artists were guests on her *Live in Central Park* album of 1999

words and music by
Sheryl Crow and Jeff Trott

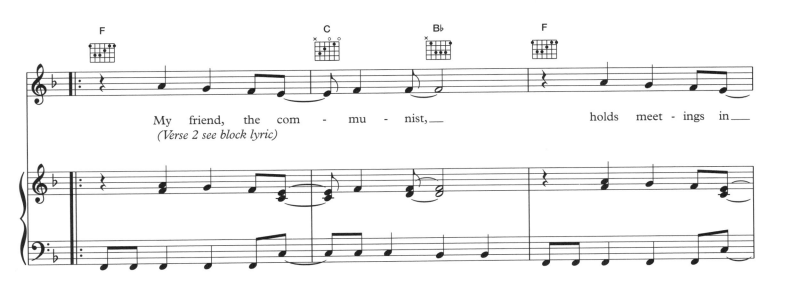

My friend, the com - mu - nist,___
(Verse 2 see block lyric)
holds meet - ings in___

___ his R.___ V.___ I can't___ af - ford___ his gas.___

So I'm stuck here watch - ing T. __ V.

I'm_____ gon-na soak up the sun,___ I'm gon-na tell ev-'ry-one

__ to light - en up._____ I'm gon-na tell 'em that

I've_____ got no one to blame._ For ev-'ry-time I feel

Verse 2
I don't have digital
I don't have didley squat
It's not having what you want
It's wanting what you've got

Verse 4
Don't have no master suite
But I'm still the king of me
You have a fancy ride, but baby
I'm the one who was the key

Shoulda, Woulda, Coulda

words and music by
Beverley Knight and Craig Wiseman

highest chart position **10**
release date **18th February 2002**
did you know The rising R&B star claims that there are two very important things she always takes on tour with her – vitamin pills, to keep her energy levels up and lipgloss

♩ = 76

Peo-ple say that to-geth-er we were both sides____ of the same coin,__

that we would shine like__ Ve-nus in a clear night sky._____ We thought our love

__ could ov - er-come the cir - cum-stan - ces,_____ but my__ am-bi-

- tion would-n't al - low__ for com-pro - mise._____

- der, _____ won-der what I'm gon-na do. __ 'Should-a would-a could-a' can't change your mind. _____

'Should-a would-a could-a' means I'm out of time. 'Should-a would-a could-a' can't change your _____

mind. _____ Oh, _____ can't change your mind. _____

People ask how it feels
To live the kind of life others dream about
I tell them everybody gotta face their highs and lows
And in my life there's a love that I put aside
'Cause I was busy loving something else
So for every little thing you hold on to
You've got to let something else go

Something To Talk About

words and music by
Damon Gough

highest chart position **28**
release date **10th June 2002**

did you know Badly Drawn Boy (a.k.a. Damon Gough) began recording music after meeting Andy Votel in Manchester and setting up the Twisted Nerve label together. But he came to renown first by appearing on the U.N.K.L.E. album *Psyence Fiction*, alongside such luminaries as Thom Yorke of Radiohead, and Richard Ashcroft of the Verve

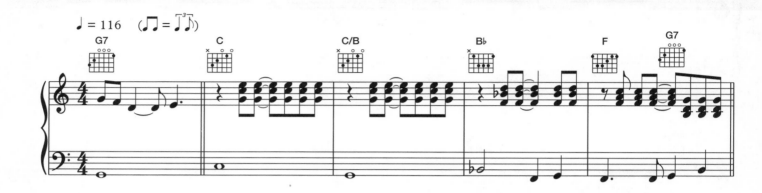

I've been dream-ing of the things I've learned__ a-bout__ a boy__

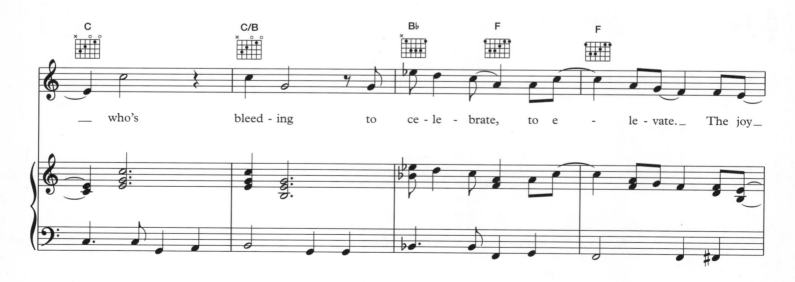

__ who's bleed-ing to ce-le-brate, to e - le-vate.__ The joy__

I've been dreaming
Of the things I learned about a boy
Who's leaving nothing else to chance again
You've got to let me in
Or let me out

What If

words and music by
Steve Mac and Wayne Hector

highest chart position 6
release date 26th November 2001
did you know Kate's first acting job
was in a Sugar Puffs commercial
dancing with the Honey Monster

Here I stand___ a-lone with this weight up-on___ my heart, and it
(See block lyric)

will not go___ a - way.___ In my head I keep on look-ing back,

right back to the start, won-drin' what it was that made you change. Well I

tried but I had to draw___ the line, and still this ques-tion keeps on spin-nin' in___ my

take it back, would you still be mine?__ 'Cos I tried, but I had to draw__ the

line, and still this ques-tion keeps on spin-nin' in__ my mind.__

What if I had ne-ver let you go?_____ Would you

be the man I used to know?__ What if I had ne-ver walked a-way?

Many roads we take
Some to joy, some to heartache
Anyone can lose the way
And if I said that we could turn it back
Right back to the start
Would you take the chance
And make the change?
Do you think how it would have been sometimes?
Do you pray that I'd never left your side?

A Woman's Worth

words and music by
Alicia Augello-Cook and Erika Rose

highest chart position **18**
release date **18th March 2002**
did you know **Alicia Keys dominated the 2002 Grammy Awards picking up no less than five awards out of the six she was nominated for. Only U2 prevented her from taking the whole half dozen**

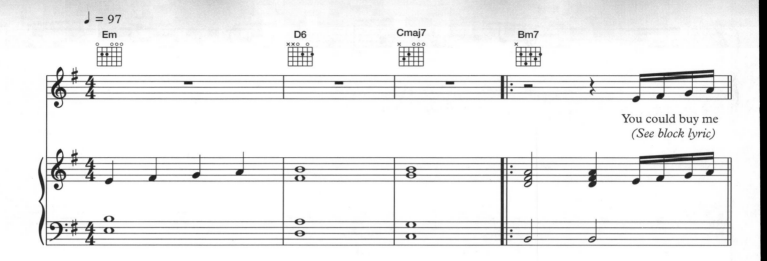

You could buy me
(See block lyric)

dia-monds, you could buy me pearls.____ Take me on a cruise a-round the world.____ (Ba-

- by, you know I'm worth it.) Din-ner lit by can-dles, run my bub-ble bath,____ make love ten-der-

If you treat me fairly
I'll give you all my goods
Treat you like a real woman should
(Baby I know you're worth it)
If you never play it, promise not to bluff
I'll hold you down when shit gets rough
(Baby I know you're worth it)
She walks the mile, makes you smile
All the while being true
Don't take for granted the passions
That she has for you

Words Are Not Enough

highest chart position 5
release date 26th November 2001
did you know Lisa has just started taking piano lessons, and can apparently play a cool rendition of ABBA's "The Winner Takes It All"

words and music by
Andreas Carlsson and Pelle Nylen

I think I heard it 'bout one thou-
(See block lyric)

- sand times or more,__ don't you bo - ther wast - ing time.

You're tell - ing me you're so much bet - - ter than be - fore, but I find it hard be - liev - ing un -

139

real - ly want_ my_ love,_____ if I'm all__ you're dream - ing_ of,___

you may find_ it tough, 'cause words are__ not e - nough._

I wouldn't ever make the same mistake again
Don't wanna be nobody's fool
I wouldn't play the losing game when you can't win
There is nothing that I'm missing
So you'd better prove me wrong

World Of Our Own

words and music by
Steve Mac and Wayne Hector

highest chart position 1
release date 18th February 2002
did you know This was the Irish boy band's 10th number one single. However, it dropped straight out of the Top Five the next week, to be replaced by Pop idol Will Young singing 'Evergreen', one of their former hits

You make me feel fun - ny when
(See block lyric)

you come a - round, yeah that's what I found out hon-ey. What am I do-ing with-out you? You make me feel

hap - py, when I leave you be - hind__ it plays on my mind__ now

Well I guess I'm ready
For settling down
And fooling around is over
And I swear that it's true
No buts or maybe's
When I'm falling down
There's always someone saves me
And girl it's you
Funny how life can
Be so surprising
I'm just realising what you do

COATES

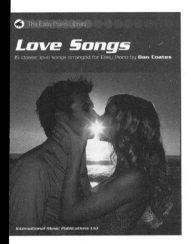
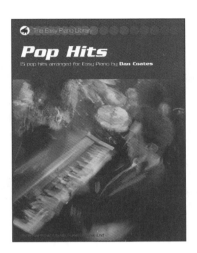
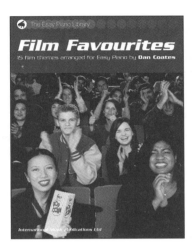
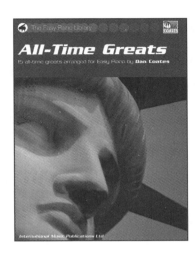

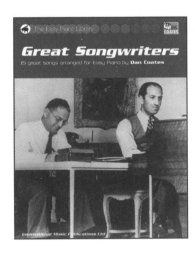

LOVE SONGS
9544A   E/PNO   ISBN: 1-84328-115-5

Angel Of Mine - Because You Loved Me - Get Here - The Greatest Love Of All - Have I Told You Lately That I Love You - I'd Lie For You (And That's The Truth) - I Turn To You - Now And Forever - The Prayer - Right Here Waiting - The Rose - Something About The Way You Look Tonight - Unbreak My Heart - When You Tell Me That You Love Me - 2 Become 1

POP HITS
9546A   E/PNO   ISBN: 1-84328-117-1

Amazed - Believe - Can't Fight The Moonlight - Genie In A Bottle - Heal The World - How Do I Live - I'll Be There For You - Kiss The Rain - Livin' La Vida Loca - Macarena - Music - Quit Playing Games With My Heart - Smooth - Swear It Again - Thank You

FILM FAVOURITES
9545A   E/PNO   ISBN: 1-84328-116-3

Batman Theme - Beautiful Stranger - Because You Loved Me - Can You Feel The Love Tonight - Can't Fight The Moonlight - Evergreen - (Everything I Do) I Do It For You - I Don't Want To Miss A Thing - Imperial March (Darth Vader's Theme) - I Will Always Love You - Somewhere My Love (Lara's Theme) - Star Wars (Main Theme) - Superman Theme - Wind Beneath My Wings

ALL TIME GREATS
9603A   E/PNO   ISBN: 1-84328-138-4

American Pie – As Time Goes By – Desperado – The Greatest Love Of All – Hotel California – Lean On Me – My Heart Will Go On – My Way – Over The Rainbow – Sacrifice – Save The Best For Last – Send In The Clowns – Stairway To Heaven – Theme From New York, New York – When You Tell Me That You Love Me

GREAT SONGWRITERS
9671A   E/PNO   ISBN: 1-84328-175-3

As Time Goes By – Bewitched – Cabaret – High Hopes – I Got Plenty O' Nuttin' – It Ain't Necessarily So – Love & Marriage – Maybe This Time – Never Met A Man I Didn't Like – Over The Rainbow – Raindrops Keep Fallin' On My Head – Send In The Clowns – Singin' In The Rain – Summertime – Tomorrow

CHRISTMAS SONGS
9790A   E/PNO   ISBN: 1-84328-309-3

All I Want For Christmas Is My Two Front Teeth - Deck The Hall - It's The Most Wonderful Time Of The Year - Jingle Bells - Let it Snow! Let it Snow! Let it Snow! - The Little Drummer Boy - Little Saint Nick - Have Yourself A Merry Little Christmas - I Believe In Santa Claus - The Most Wonderful Day Of The Year - O Christmas Tree - Rockin' Around The Christmas Tree - Rudolph, The Red-Nosed Reindeer - Santa Claus Is Comin' To Town - Sleigh Ride - The Twelve Days Of Christmas - Winter Wonderland

An expansive series of over 50 titles!

Each song features melody line, vocals, chord displays, suggested registrations and rhythm settings.

"For each title ALL the chords (both 3 finger and 4 finger) used are shown in the correct position - which makes a change!" **Organ & Keyboard Cavalcade, May 2001**

Each song appears on two facing pages eliminating the need to turn the page during performance. We have just introduced a new cover look to the series and will repackage the backlist in the same way.

Order Ref:4766A

Pick up a free Songfinder from your local Music Shop